Treading Lightly....

Small Steps Along the Path

by

L.D.B. Taylor

*~Dedicated to all those who follow
The Path~*

Second Printing, 2013

ISBN-13: 978-0615776347

ISBN-10:0615776345

Neebeep Publishing

www.neebeep.com

Preface…

Twenty-two years ago I gave birth to a baby girl. Our first born.

A short time later, a doctor who I had never seen before, though who since has become a trusted family friend, carried that oh so tiny baby girl to me. Drained, the blessed Demerol seeping through my veins, I stared up at him, and my husband, standing granite faced behind. The doctor spoke, such a kind, caring voice; a touch of woe and pain just behind it:

I believe your daughter has Down Syndrome.

My world went black then. And life transformed.

But I've written of all this before, in a previous volume entitled *Reclamation: A Heartbroken & Then I Got Better Love Story.*
The earliest memories, those I want to remember, are in its pages.
And yes those pages are filled with tears, and some freely admitted self pity and rather purple prose.

And that's okay.

Because we're all on a journey, a path; and some of us are able to stomp our way through, filled with self confidence and certainty and bravado.

And then are those, like me, who tread a bit more lightly.

Gingerly taking those steps, pondering, agonizing, over thinking; we, my friends, are the *worrierers.*
This I freely embrace; just as I freely embrace that the path I was cast upon was indeed chosen by myself; in a time past remembering and all encompassing.

Once upon a time, I believe my spirit chose to help bring life to this child of mine with Down Syndrome.
She's helped her brothers, her father, and myself along our own journeys – indeed, she has taught us so much more than we could possibly have taught her.

So, I have learned much in those twenty-two years. In addition to our daughter, my husband and I now have four loud sons: strong and healthy and unruly as boys can be.

And that baby girl of ours? Our Girl Girl, as we call her, well believe me when I say she rules our house.
She is bright and funny, sweet and obnoxious, hateful and helpful.
Her own person: willful, opinionated, strong.

All the things a girl should be.

No matter how many chromosomes she may have.

A few of our, oftimes rather faltering, steps...

Cast of Characters

The Hard Love
Perfection Lost
All Grown Up
She Thinks...
Time Flows
Asserting Yourself
Waiting
The Wilderness Path
Our Girl Is A Busy Person
Whispered Song
Of Schedules & Girls
Recipes (by Girly Girl)
A List of Cans, Cant's, & Probably Won'ts
Girly Girl Graduates
Girly Girl's Resume
Girly Girl's Resume Part II
The Wilderness Path II
Empty
Hunkering Down
Good Day Prayers
And The Dance Continues.

About The Author

This is the hour of lead

Remembered, if outlived

As freezing persons recollect the snow –

First chill, then stupor;

Then the letting go.

~Emily Dickinson

~*Cast of Characters*~
The Star!
Our Girl, the Spitfire

Full time Princess, Dancer, Singer, Web Surfer. (Gotta keep track of that last one.)

Definite leanings toward some type of espionage (ie. she is crafty, sneaky, yet *appears* innocent!)

Me:
Overwhelmed & understaffed Mom of 5. Writer. Treadmill wary & frightened by the oddly flexible yoga lady on the dvd.

The optimist sees the rose and not its thorns; the pessimist stares at the thorns, oblivious to the rose.
~ Kahlil Gibran

Scott:

The Dad. Self-sufficient. Refuses to admit to being overwhelmed.

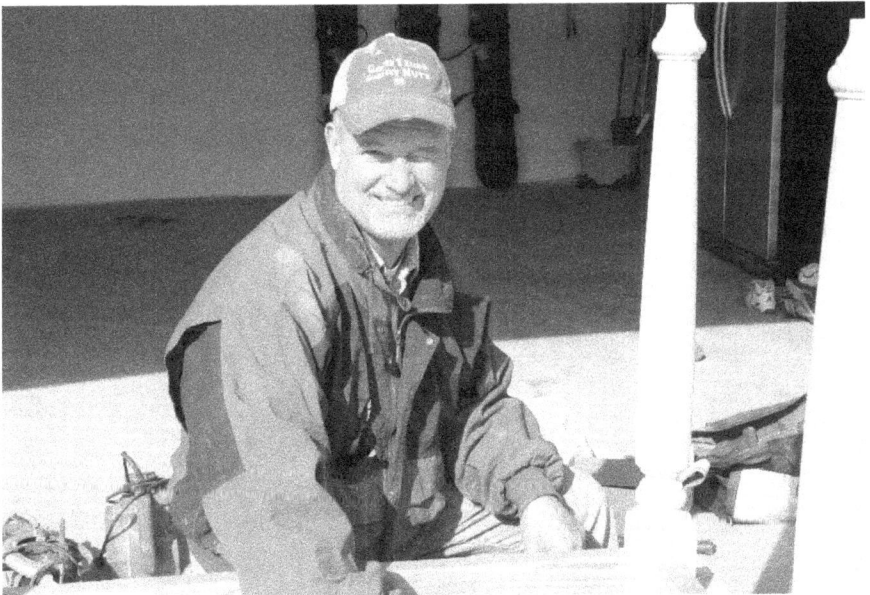

Brothers:
There are four.
All but three are now bigger than Our Girl, though she still rules with an iron hand and the loudest indignant screech west of the Mississippi.

Son&Heir

Curlytop

Little Bit & Coyote

The Hard Love

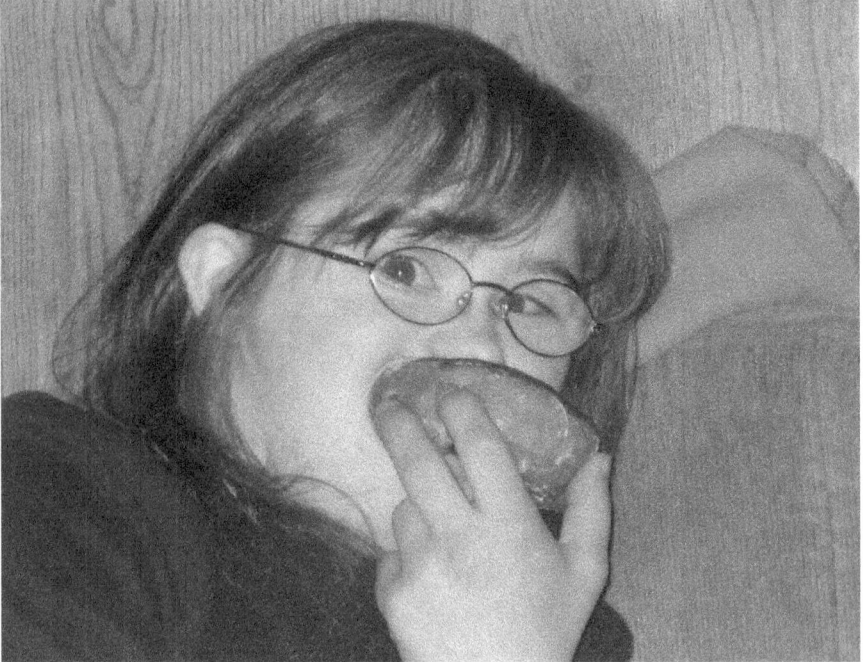

Before you arrived the love was easy.

I felt you moving, knew that you were already there, yet still connected to that other; the universe, the blessed be, the God we're all connected to; and never more so than we are children. I knew the stars danced within your eyes, though I couldn't yet see those eyes; (they are green, and brown and sparkling.) I knew your body was formed of sacred stuff, and it lived within Me.

When you were born it was hard. Pain, fear, blood, my thinking it would never end while knowing in my somewhere mind it would. And then you were there -

from where? I believe I know now, though I have no proof. Just belief And faith. Both hard concepts to keep up day by day, every day; so many days.

And then I discovered you weren't quite who I'd imagined. Were going to be, *supposed to be.*

The words Down Syndrome plunged into my world with a jolt; huge and overwhelming. That was the hardest. But still I loved you, even when I didn't. Even when I wondered who you were and why this had happened to you; why it had happened to me.

Loving you anew, again, still, was hard. But sometimes that which seems the hardest becomes the easiest, once we enter the path. Once we began to tread, step by step, day by day, yet again.

And today - nearly 22 years later. I see the star stuff in your eyes daily. I hear the heavens dance to your laugh. And I know the hard stuff is what creates us; what leads us up and along that path, down the deepest hill, and upward once more.

Sounds simple doesn't it.

The simple is love; hidden by the hard.

A pessimist sees only the dark side of the clouds, and mopes; a philosopher sees both sides, and shrugs; an optimist doesn't see the clouds at all – he's walking on them.

~Leonard Louis Levinson

Perfection Lost….

Perhaps you don't know many perfect people…

Neither do I.

But once upon a time, around 22 years ago, I was very nearly perfect.

Do you find that surprising? Because I do. But it's true. I was the perfect size, I had the perfect college GPA, a perfect marriage, and we were building the perfect house because I was pregnant with our first and, obviously, perfect child.

I went into labour during the wee hours of the night. This was also perfect, because it's what always happens on all the perfectly fabulous old movies. And later, after much struggle and pain, blood and fear, (because, really, that's what it takes to enter into this world of ours. And perhaps what it takes to survive in it), I gave birth perfectly; without any pain killers or medications. Just as the Lamaze class which Scott and I had taken had taught us to; as we were supposed to do (all the books and magazines had told us so.) Naturally we'd had perfect class attendance.

And when our baby girl was born? Well she was perfect. Very nearly. You see, as I looked at her, I found myself thinking imperfect thoughts. Not the thoughts I'd imagined a new mother would think. Do perfect mothers think their baby girls resemble Winston Churchill? I didn't know. So I choose to blame it on the Demerol shot they'd just given me to as they repaired the physical damage childbirth can do, and left it at that.

My perfect world lasted around another hour.

And then the paediatrician came in. Our Girl had Down Syndrome. No one's fault, the odds had been against this ever happening. But it does happen, and to young, perfect mothers. Mothers who read all the books, and take their prenatal vitamins; who are on time to every doctor appointment, and eat well.

So - *Perfection Lost.*

I couldn't forgive the loss of being perfect, (though of course I knew I'd never really been perfect at all.) I couldn't forgive God and I couldn't forgive myself. Such total failure demanded heavy penance and severe punishment.

So I pushed God away. No doubt I had never seemed religious in the world's eyes, and I'm not religious in the traditional sense. But I am spiritual, a seeker, a deep believer; and all of that, from the moment the words Down Syndrome came so quietly from that doctor's lips, became alien.

I had been an intellectual, a scholar; and those traits, so innate to me, such a large part of who I was, were ripped away as well. Ripped away by God and my own imperfection. I couldn't read the books I normally read (will she be able to read them?) I didn't watch the television programs I had always watched (*will she ever watch Masterpiece Theatre?*) I couldn't bear to be near happy people (*why do they get to be happy?*), and I couldn't bear anyone who seemed sad *(what do they have to be sad about?)*

But this is supposed to be about forgiveness. And I did forgive, very slowly.

After even more seeking and reading and thinking (over thinking: my weakness and strength.) After giving birth a second time to a baby boy, and months of looking in the mirror and wondering who that poor, overwhelmed woman staring back at me *was*; wondering whose house I was living in, filled with baby toys and crying children; dirty diapers and too many bottles.

I don't believe time heals, but it does dull the pain. Time allows that sharp ache to ease, as the mind wraps itself around a new reality, eventually finding peace and yes, even joy in it. Eventually I was able to realize that there wasn't really anyone to forgive, because no one had been at fault.

My spiritual self grew to understand there is indeed a purpose, a plan, a journey each soul must take and that this journey, like it or not, was mine. And my practical self (if indeed I possess such a thing) realized, amazed, that I did kinda like this journey. That this baby girl, this busy toddler in pink, this vibrant little girl, and now this young woman with an attitude and spitfire personality is an irreplaceable part of my journey, just as Scott, and her brothers (four now), and I are a part of hers.

To forgive is to understand, and I grew to understand that forgiveness is possible. Even toward myself.

When one door of happiness closes, another opens; but often we look so long at the closed door that we do not see the pen which has been opened for us.

~Helen Keller

All Grown Up

The Moment I realized I was a Grown Up...

I had given birth for the first time. It was hard.

Childbearing is not, as some you have you believe, a gathering of friends who sing kumbiya while everyone stitches a lovely quilt, drinks herbal tea, and passes around a plate of suspicious looking brownies - including you, between Lamaze *hee hee hee and ho ho ho's.*

 Childbirth is about pain and blood and fear, sometime a lot of fear. It's your husband (or whoever you helper, your coach is - I hope you have one. If not you can call me), assuring that you're "nearly there" - and during that first labour you believe him.

It's those subsequent times you know he's lying through his teeth, and you squeeze his hand just a tad harder; hearing his words through gritted teeth *"No nails! No nails!"* coming from an amazingly long way off. It isn't called labour for nothing. No doubt many have said that before.

Of course women have done it for centuries. With help from other, empathetic and wincing, women. A damp rag held to their forehead, a stick thrust between their teeth. Lying down, squatting, hanging onto a doorway, or a chair, or their sister/mother/friend. Straining and praying to get that baby born alive, and if possible, to stay alive too; so they will be able to see and love what they have helped bring forth. Truly they have become a sort of doorway, from that world beyond into this world of ours.

Following that first, hard birth. I settled back into a soft bed. Nurses to care for me. My husband and family smiling over the baby; this person, who had miraculously emerged from Me, and yet not from me. And I was exhausted and given meds and made comfortable. I was cared for and congratulated, pampered and fed.

And then, an hour or so later, I grew up.

When the paediatrician came in carrying my baby girl. When I saw Scott's face - pale stone beneath his new, pink brimmed "It's a girl!" baseball cap. When the doctor began to list off all the things which were right, which were proper and good about Our Girl, (*this is what they tell them to do. He did a perfect job.*)

And when I, always suspicious, always thinking, despite the lovely Demerol flowing throughout my body - there to numb the pain - when I interrupted him:

"Just tell me!" I said. Thinking: "*Well she doesn't have two heads, she isn't missing an arm or any fingers, are her insides wrong? Is her heart missing? Will she die in an hour? What?*

Just tell me!"

 So he did. Down Syndrome. And - it was so strange - my world went black. Utterly dark. Blinded, I reared up in the bed; they tried to ease me back down. (*I've never understood why. What did they think I was going to do? Blast through the wall? Rampage down the hospital corridors? Run screaming into the night?*)

But it was day. A fine morning in April after a night's rain. Sun streamed in the hospital windows, yet I sat up in the bed, seeing black space, literally space - with billions of stars ahead. Bright suns I could nearly touch with one outstretched hand.

"I think your daughter has Down Syndrome."

And that, was when I grew up.

For In much wisdom is much grief: and he that increaseth knowledge increaseth sorrow.

Ecclesiastes 1:18

She Thinks

(She is always thinking.)

Physical Beauty? What is it? Who decides?

Naturally it can open doors, though how long those door remain open is the question.

The beautiful candidate, the beautiful model or actress; though we all know (suspect?), the not so beautiful character actress or the girl hiding out in the corner with her nose stuck in a book has more talent and imagination.

That candidate who isn't quite so photogenic but more qualified.

Beauty is subjective

Many people have told us Our Girl is beautiful. She believes herself a Beautiful Princess, and I'm ok with that.

I figure being the mother of a Beautiful Princess is a pretty good gig.

Others have glanced her way; glanced away.

That extra chromosome dancing around in each of her cells making them uncomfortable, uncertain: *How do I act? What do I say?*

Glance back: I catch their eye and smile. They smile back; usually.

"She's beautiful." They gaze with that wide smile at her; but mostly at me. As though describing a sculpture, a painting, a doe standing poised, ready to flee. Flying nearly; those graceful leaps, dark feet held aloft, knees flexed and stretching.

And Our Girl smiles and tells them her name, perhaps shakes their hand.

Has a door been opened?

If her hair wasn't long and flowing, if she weren't so short and cute and friendly, would they recognize her beauty then?

Or would it all stop at that first eye catch, that first quick (false, false, false) smile, then advert those eyes and move away. Leaving Our Girl no new person to introduce herself to, no hand to shake.

Doors open and close.

Beauty fades. Skin lines, softens, droops. Bright eyes grow cloudy, scathing wit may dull, a heaviness in the chest when arising, the quick slowness of another day. The echoing silence of a door slamming shut.

Look beneath the door.

The light flowing out is truly beautiful. Those doors such light opens remain so: wide and welcoming, beckoning others to follow.

Our Girl's light beauty is so bright it burns the eyes.

If you recognize it; if you're brave and true enough to strain your eyes and gaze through it, the beauty is there.

Flowing wild and free behind the character actress's broad nose or budging eyes, behind the qualified candidate's tense smile, behind the book which provides that insecure beauty such an excellent wall.

Beyond the thinned skin; veined, age spotted hands.

Behind and within and hovering about that dancing extra chromosome. I was never beautiful. I was average; less than, never expecting more. This is what I always heard and knew. I hadda push that door open, wedging in a foot. Grit your teeth, ignore the pain, keep on.

Yet Our Girl is a Beautiful Princess. And it opens doors and closes them.

She will not be a lawyer. She will never have children.

Yet she will dance in the light; and believe, believe, believe.

Her beauty blows the doors off their hinges.

The light floods through, allowing all to dance: warmed and lifted.

In the depth of winter, I finally learned that within me there lay an invincible summer.
                        ~Albert Camus

Time Flows….

And time continues on, as we all know it will; to both our chagrin and hope.

No matter how wistfully we hope it won't, so matter how hard we pray.
Times flows, and we flow with it: we age, our children grow, loved ones pass on. So we come to realize, and, if we're lucky, to accept, that life is *just this:* flowing.

Moving on. All of us in the river never-ending; together and at home, yet alone and in a strange land, all at once. Being taken along by the warm current; cool eddies meeting us along the way. The occasional waterfall seeming to appear from nowhere engulfing us and washing us along.

Till we arrive: water cleansed, worn, abandoned and breathing hard.

Breathe hard. Allow the water to cleanse.

Know the strange land will prove itself familiar, and you are never alone.

Twenty years from now you will be more disappointed by the things that you didn't do than by the ones you did do. So throw off the bowlines. Sail away from the safe harbor. Catch the trade winds in your sails. Explore. Dream. Discover.
~Mark Twain

The Difficult Art of Asserting Yourself

The times I have asserted myself....

I haven't always been the best at asserting myself.

I'm the type who gets mad, loses her temper, (my boys call this *Mom freaking out*), and then turns the air blue; because, as my mother always said, *I can swear like a drunken sailor when so inclined.*

Asserting yourself is different from ~~freaking out~~ *getting angry*.

Asserting yourself is letting someone know how you feel in a strong, yet calm and rational manner, then standing your ground.

This is a time I asserted myself:

Girly Girl's school bus was late. 20 minutes, then 30. I called "Transportation", they spoke to the bus driver via their radio and were told that she would be there "soon." Another 15 minutes passes, no Girly Girl.

I call Transportation. (They are very nice people at Transportation.) They called the bus driver again and were again told she would be there "soon."

Another 20 minutes or so passes.

I am now totally ~~pissed off~~ *angry*. The people at Transportation aren't too thrilled either. They are talking to me on one line, and gripping at their bus driver on the other.
I consider calling the police and reporting my Girl as stolen by a crazed bus driver.
This continues for around 30-45 minutes. Finally the bus pulls up in front of our house.

Girly Girl disembarks, accompanied by the driver and the "helper" (this is a special ed bus you must remember, there is always a "helper.")
They come to the door. The driver begins making excuses. I (calmly) hold up one hand and say "I can't talk to you about this right now."

(Now wasn't that mature? I didn't even begin clawing her face or anything!)

Said bus driver (hereafter referred to as "idiot in dingle bobble hat") keeps gabbling. Making lame excuses:
She had other kids to deliver, other schools to pick up from, she forgot to bring Girly Girl home during her first afternoon run, then, not wanting to be late, went onto three different schools, delivering those children home on time.

I stare at her, unable to say anything. Then, the ~~bi...,~~ idiot in dingle bobble hat, whirls on her heel, flaps her hand dismissively toward me, and, all hoity toity and filled with self righteousness huffs "Well, if you won't even converse with me!!" and marches off.

Now I'm way ~~pissed~~ angry.

My boys, who've been hovering with antenna out, all eyes and ears by the front door, scatter.

I step further out onto the porch and ROAR:

(Really, imagine a ginormous commanding voice, like Darth Vader meets Captain Jon Luc Picard on steroids. Squared.)

"DON'T YOU TURN YOUR BACK ON ME!"

Idiot in dingle bobble hat and Helper freeze. They both turn around, slack jawed. Pure terror in their eyes. I've never seen anything like it.
It was great.

Then I started. I ranted, I raved, I lectured and not once did I turn the air blue!
(This, my friends, was a total miracle.)

I finished, took our Girl into the house where her brothers proceeded to make her a triple stack of her favorite "cheese chips" and two diet cokes. She was tearful & frightened, and kept telling me they'd missed her house.

I filed a complaint with the district of course.

We drove Girly Girl to school ourselves for the next week, till Christmas break.

And after Christmas Girly Girl wound up with a different bus driver.

Which was nice. Because I would have hated to have torn the Idiot in dingle bobble hat's dingle bobble off and shoved it down her throat.

That wouldn't have been mature and assertive at all, now would it?

Waiting

She said she would call in two weeks.

Two weeks can either be a short or very long time. When you're on holiday, two weeks zip past in the blink of an eye. One day you're just venturing out, roadmap in hand, everything you've packed clean and fresh. And suddenly, it's over; your roadmap handled into a wrinkled, unintelligible paper-cloth; the place names so vibrant in memory, creased and softened, your luggage light, the dirty laundry bag budging ominously. You know what you're in for when you arrive home.

I waited, we waited, two weeks.

Without new sights to divert me, lacking any type of map at all; though this was new territory, and terrifying.

Terrain crafted with deep valleys and jagged cliffs which I was expected to tread calmly, clenching tight to Faith's hand.

(Don't tell anyone: but sometimes Faith's hands are slippery, and all too often It threatened to go on alone, abandoning me in the wilderness.)

And so I walked the Wilderness Path, not for the first time, and not for the last. I walked and grasped at Faith's slippery hand and waited for the phone call which may, or may not, guide me home.

Isn't it strange, but I've forgotten her name.
Her card stayed in my wallet for years, transferred from
the old to the new along with driver's license, insurance
card, a bit of prayer cloth, a few coins. (I never have cash.)
But I know her hair was reddish brown and curly, her face
smooth and freckled, she wore glasses and seemed happy
and confident in her small office.
The building she worked in was huge, with wide winding
corridors; wonderfully clean. There were many windows;
shining and clear.

(*But such windows can be deceptive; though their view is
sun filled and enticing, they are impenetrable. Impossible
to break through, though you slam your body against
them again and again. The sunshine beckons just outside,
teasing you. Knowing you are upon the wilderness path,
and must follow it to the end.*)

Finally, when I'd trudged the path to the point where one
imagines with sure certainly it has no ending. When the
pain within my stomach had turned to a constant tight
churning, and I could focus on nothing but the small steps
my feet were taking; though always whenever I managed
a quick glance upward I found myself in the same spot.
Finally, finally that phone rang and I ran with it into the
bathroom, holding tight to Faith's hand now.

Whispering the long memorized *Memorare* in my mind, again and again. Pressing my back against the wall (would it remain solid, or crumble into ruins?) and *listening, listening.*

This is... she began.

Though I recognized her voice as well as my mother's. I clenched Faith's hand hard, digging my nails in, knowing It could take it.

I tried to speak but she continued, quickly, *Calling with good news!"*

And I crumpled, sliding down the firm wall, Faith easing the way.
Everything looks perfect. No chromosomal problems at all.
I'm sure I replied, though I've no idea what I said. (No doubt Faith remembers...)

Would you like to know whether it's going to be a boy or a girl?

And it was a boy!

The Wilderness Path I

Jesus said, *"Let the little children come to me, and do not hinder them, for the kingdom of heaven belongs to such as these."* Matthew 19:14

Often now, the pain comes on suddenly.

It never fails to catch me by surprise; the sudden heaviness, the dark cloud, the all consuming knowledge that this is what I have to face. And it will *be*, and *is*, and will *never leave.*

And then I remember, after several moments, half a second, three hours, that never is *now*. That all is one and there is a purpose, though so very much remains hidden still.

Girly Girl has Down Syndrome. It will never leave her body. This June she will graduate from "her college"; and from then on every minute of her every day will be mine to help fill and fulfill. *Forever After.*
Until I die.
Unthinkable...*me* dying...

I don't die. People like me don't die. We scream and cry and rage. We wander in the desert and find a path back. We pause, we think, we plan...and then we gaze back upon our hard forged path, and find joy, lingering there in the shadows.

But eventually the body wears out.
And then where will my Girly Girl be?

She has her brothers. Three young men and a young boy. Eventually four strong men, hopefully with a purpose and faith deeply engrained. Fine spirits; filled with empathy, courage, and love.
But are they their Sister's "keepers"?

Is it fair to…(*can I say it*)…to *burden* them with their Sister's welfare?
What of their wives, their children, their lives?

Perhaps it is. And I *feel* I know why.

It's been said, so many times, that we are spirits manifest in bodies. We are star stuff (I love that phrase!) We are embodiers of the eternal light. We are a reflection and a part of God.

He The Blessed Be.

As a Quaker I know the light shines in everyone. You can see it if you care to.

My favorite part of the film ET was the idea of *Heartlight*. Lovely term isn't it? And the image of the *Heartlight*; existing in each of us. We are all connected, all part of the greater whole. All on our own journey through this life, this "EarthSchool", (another favorite phrase.)

But why? To evolve, to learn, to become at one with ourselves, others, and the *Blessed Be* who somehow granted us that first spark of light.

So, should our Girly Girl expect her brothers to care for her, to watch over & protect her when I am gone?

Yeal, I think so.

Because she is a part of them and they of her. Because, I believe, each one of their spirits chose this path before.

(When is before? I don't know. In heaven? A pre-existence? Before incarnating into the body? Honestly just the word Before is enough for me.)

Girly Girl's brothers chose their paths, chose the burden and joy of having a sister with Down Syndrome; just as Scott and I chose to have a daughter with Down Syndrome; just as Our Girl herself chose to face a harder path this time around.
The lessons she has to learn, insurmountable to me.

Yet she travels along them with glad courage. Such a strong Heartlight.

For Joy fills *her* wilderness path with a warm and welcoming glow, lighting her way.

Our Girl in High School, with one of her wonderful teachers!

Our Girl Is A Busy Person...

She writes lists. Mostly library lists, Christmas Lists, & Birthday Lists. And she gives them to ME.

Library Lists I receive every other day or so. They usually contain forty to fifty items.

Christmas Lists begin the day after her birthday in late April, Birthday Lists begin (naturally) the day after Christmas.

I receive these lists in the form of what I call *Missives From Above.*

Girly Girl folds the missive twice. (For those in the know about such things, one hot dog fold, followed by one hamburger fold.)

She then floats (or some may say *throws*) the missive from the family room balcony or foyer hallway. Then she announces the delivery of her message to the world.

 (There is no doubt in my mind that Girly Girl was quite a successful town crier in a former life.)

Girly Girl: *MOM THERE'S A NOTE!*

Me (occupied in doing something no doubt terribly important): *I know sweetie, I get in it in a minute.*

Girly Girl: *MOM. THE NOTE!*

Me (still otherwise occupied): I ***know sweetie! I'll get it in a minute!*** .

This "conversation" may repeat as many as 10 to 20 times.

Really.

To be honest the endearment "sweetie" makes its exit during round six or so. The entire trying episode usually ends by my stopping whatever important task I was involved in, walking over and retrieving the flippin' note.

Both Birthday & Christmas Lists always include:

-A Pink Refrigerator (which evidently every person requires in his or her bedroom)

-Diet coke

-A laptop (pink)

-Pepsi, Pepsi, Pepsi,

-And two to four pages of closely written movie and book titles. *Scooby Doo* and *Jackie Chan Adventure* dvds always prominently represented.

Obtaining the *Scooby Doos* isn't a problem, but the *Jackie Chans* are available only at a few places, at an amazing price.

Which of course I'm not willing to pay.

Still Girly Girl continues to ~~throw~~ float down her missives.

She has great faith in her system.

I suppose there aren't many Town Crier positions available these days.

Perhaps she's destined for a career with the Postal Service.

Whispered Song

On Loss...

During pregnancy, the thought of the baby growing within forms in your mind. Brown hair or blond, dark or fair eyes. Chubby fingers and toes; ten of each (*and we count 'em quick as that baby gets born, just to make sure.*)

Sometimes what we've imagined doesn't appear. The magic fails, the image is cruelly replaced, the faith falters.

And the loss is devastating.

You mourn for the child you imagined. Surely she was there – you could see and feel her so clearly. And when you spoke to her, sang to her, told silly stories to her couldn't you hear her voice answering? Wasn't it her, whispering love songs to you as you slept; telling you when it was her time to finally emerge and meet you- face to face.

With a rush of pain, using strength you certainly can't possess that child is born.

And you look at her in wonder and amazement, and a growing awareness, keen through even the pain haze and blood and fear that something, *something* isn't what you'd imagined.

And you are told. Are positive.

And... how amazing, the sky becomes black without a single star to steer by.

You mourn the loss.

She will not read the books you love. She will not go to college, live independently, marry, have children. She will not travel to Rome with a group of friends, stroll the city, gelato in hand, adding to her knowledge, her spirit; soaking in the history, the smell and sounds. Closing her eyes and imagining the Ancients there, right there, where she is standing.

She won't understand the how or the why of doing such things. And if you try to explain she'll smile at you *Oh Mom,* and glance toward the restaurant nearby or tell you her feet hurt.

Other people won't understand her language as you will. The loss will be keen then.

(You'll remember your mother's wail at her birth *"But I won't be able to talk to her*!

Oh how that will echo, till you stop your ears and squeeze your eyes tight.)

The Loss will overwhelm you and ache as you watch the girl you'd imagined fade from the very corner of your mind's eye. The one who was taller than you. Pretty. Confident as you could never be.

Can you see her still? The one you lost *(the one who never was.)* She's at college now, that girl. Her hair is long and thick with wild pink and purple streaks. She dances and studies and wears jewel toned "hippie clothes" with a casual shrug you could never manage.

Fading... fading; whispering love songs to you as she trails away.

And your Girly Girl is here. And she wants a coke and her long dark hair needs washed and you are the one to help with both.

So you help her. And you answer her *knock knock* joke for the ten millionth time and listen to her music blaring from beneath her closed bedroom door.

She hugs you every morning; *You're the best mom ever.* And you close your eyes and listen, hearing a bit of the love songs you once shared. Sensing in this short little stinkerbum Girly Girl just a bit of the one you'd imagined she'd be: the temper, the independent streak, the dancing, the casual *What do I care what they think* spirit.

Loss overwhelms and you lie empty. Loss remains, and aches. Becoming a part of you. Forcing you to fill in the edges, plaster the cracks, pull your sorry self offa that floor and move on.

And, one fine day, the imaginary never was child becomes recognizable in the here and now real child.

Loss helps you see they are one, and always were. That tall, beautiful, independent, spirit is *right here*: in this little spitfire with an extra chromosome. *(And isn't it amazing what attitude that chromosome carries with it.)*

Loss has broken your heart; and has widened it.

Opening your eyes; sharpening your ears.

And you *know...* those whispered love songs, the silly stories, the tiny voice of the soaring Old Spirit overflowing with knowledge and peace, are right here and always were.

Listen now to the song...

Isn't it lovely?

Of Schedules & Girls

Our Girl has a schedule. She is now 21, in her last year of "her college."

This is the time we've been worrying about since she was born.

What do we do now?

Girly Girl isn't worried.

She has plans to go to New York, work at the Natural History Museum, & ride around with Teddy Roosevelt on Texas when the joint comes alive at night.

When I asked her how she plans to get to New York she replied *"At the Airport."*

The Girl is nothing if not self sufficient.

Her school schedule has always been quite interesting and diverse. She's had several "jobs" around the city, some of which she loved, some she coulda done without. (I rather suspect those establishments lacked vending machines.)

She goes bowling, shopping, to the gym, the library, cooking class, and to her "job site." Wednesday is library day. Girly Girl loves the library. She has visited the library at least once a week ever since she can remember.

When she was in preschool her teacher's main complaint was that all Girly Girl wanted to do was "read" books.

Yet Wednesday, school library day, is currently the day she consistently refuses to go to school.

We have literally attempted to drag the Girl out of bed.

She's strong.

Even at 6 a.m.

She whines, she cries, she says she's sick, has cramps, her stomach and/or head hurt, or indignantly announces:

"There's No School Today! My Teacher Told Me!"

Later, in the afternoon, she's been known to come down from her "lair", and smugly sing out *"I fooled you."*

She's such a little stinker.

Yet we continue to wonder, *why does* she so dislike Wednesdays?

I have consulted her teacher about this. She's stumped as well.

I think it's because Girly Girl knows it's Scott's day off and she doesn't want to miss out on anything. Like stopping at a fast food joint for lunch.

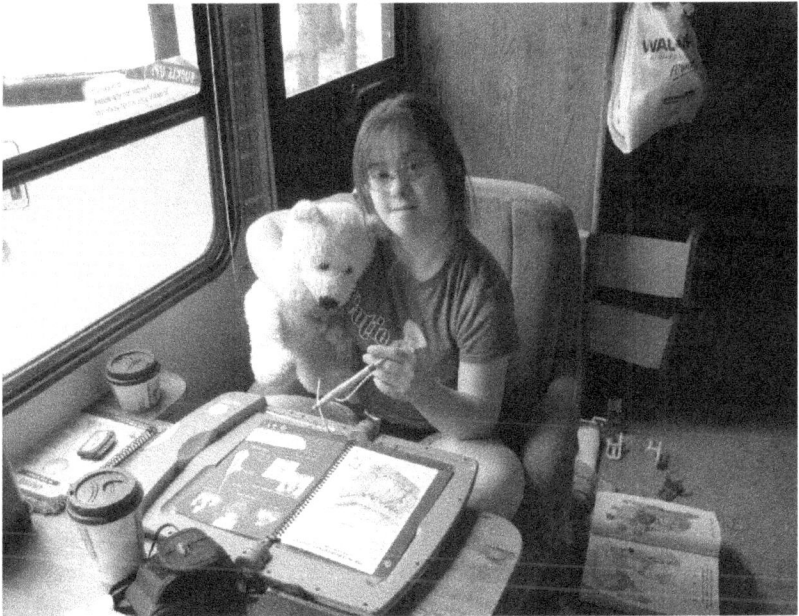

How Girly Girl camps

I *know* Girly Girl.

She may fool other people with her *"I'm a just a sweet thing. People with Down Syndrome don't always understand like other people do."*

And that's true enough. But *Our Girl* has a streak of manipulative deviousness in her that is deep and wide. (Lord knows where she got it.)

She thinks and plans. She makes lists, she sniffs out the diet coke when I'm sure I have it well hidden, and manages to get into her closet to "rearrange it" after Scott has installed a combination lock on a heavy latch sunk through to a stud with 3 inch screws.

And she graduates this summer...

We are in such trouble.

(I'm thinking I should put the local airport on alert.)

The deeper sorrow carves into your being the more joy you can contain.
~Kahlil Gibran

Recipes

Developed by Girly Girl some years ago.

(Patents pending.)

POPCORN SOUP

Pop a package of low fat microwave popcorn your parents have thoughtfully purchased.

Discover said popcorn is not "buttery" enough.

Melt an entire stick of butter.

Add to popcorn, stir thoroughly.

Melt a second entire stick of butter.

Add to popcorn, stir thoroughly.

Begin melting a third entire stick of butter – raising busy mother's suspicions by running microwave too long.

Said mother enters kitchen, picks up large "popcorn bowl" containing popcorn, and nearly drops it while discovering bowl is amazingly heavy (for popcorn.)

Distraught mother gazes into popcorn bowl to discover drenched popcorn puffs literally swimming in sloshing bowl of hot butter.

Distraught mother throws popcorn out. Outraged daughter stomps upstairs to room and slams door.

SOGGY MAC & CHEESE

Open box of mac and cheese.

Fill pot with whatever amount of water desired.

Toss in entire contents of mac and cheese. Stir. Turn burner to low.

Abandon kitchen to watch TV while entire mess cooks, leaving Distraught Mother to find it (hopefully) minutes later.

A List of Cans, Can'ts, and Probably Won'ts

Ah Girly Girl

(And yes she is known by other names: Princess, The Princess, Miss Priss, Angel Mae, as well as *That Sneaky Little Thing Who Swiped The Last Diet Coke.*

She has Down Syndrome

Suffice to say it is a developmental disability, and it won't go away.

But that doesn't mean Girly Girl isn't amazingly capable of many things.

So here I present a partial list of things she can and cannot do:

Girly Girl CAN:

~Sneak off with the last can of diet coke right under your nose. No idea how she does it.

~Manipulate people. She would be a great CIA agent if it weren't for the possible distractions of interesting shops and restaurants.

~Dance. She can step-dance, hip-hop, ballerina twirl till she falls over, and possibly break dance.

~Sing - louder than you could ever imagine possible.

~Clean her room and fold her laundry perfectly. (Really - it looks as though a machine did it.) *When* she's in the mood of course.

~Make me laugh. She says the funniest things. (And I feel certain they're all planned)

~Bowl. We're thinking of taking her professional. (Or at least getting her her own pink, sparkly ball.)

~Give a quick retort to her brothers whenever they bug her. (*Take a bath hippie!* is her current favorite.)

~Read. The girl is a reading machine. Always has been.

~Compose frightening notes and float them down off the loft onto my desk. (Or head.)

Said notes say things like *"They're In The House"*, and *"They're Back. Check My Closet."*

These never fail to totally. Freak. Me. Out.

~Put together an outfit so eclectic it looks as though I created it.

~Catch a fish within five minutes of her pole touching water.

(Really, it's uncanny. And quite frustrating to her brothers.)

What she *can't* do:

~Drive a car. We gave her her chance with her Barbie Car. She immediately drove it straight into the wall. Twice.

~Work well with money.

Obviously the girl's of royal blood as she never carries the stuff and is a bit confused by the point of it.

(When one discovers something one desires upon a shop shelf, one simply pockets it and assumes one's minions will take care of the pesky details.)

~Talk slowly enough so that everyone can properly understand her. Leonardo had his backwards handwriting; Girly Girl has her speed talking.

Ask her a question and chances are, (*if* she acquiesces to oblige you with an answer), she will reply with such a blurred whirl of words you will blink for a moment and reply *"Oh."*

If you are so bold as to demand a repeat of her answer she will do one of two things:

1- *(And this occurs only upon her rare, patient days),* repeat it more slowly for you, you poor sod. Then, if she's being extraordinarily obliging, she will spell it and stare at you pointedly.

Or *(and most likely),*

2- Gaze at you in abject pity, pocket her pilfered diet coke and swiss roll and make her escape.

Hmmm...

Yup - that's it. That is all I can think of that Girly Girl can't do.

Girly Girl Graduates

And Girly Girl graduates.

She is 22. She graduates from "her college."

A safe place where she has attended dances and barbecues, and raided the junk food machines so conveniently located right outside her classroom, with quarters pilfered from her brother's piggy bank. (She did show remorse; though I suspect, only at being caught.)

She was in Class 6, along with other special needs kids – all on their bumpy road toward adulthood.

Girly Girl is an adult child. I suppose we all are, but it's that extra chromosome which makes her just a bit more special.

So she wears a hat and gown, and marches across the stage (*why we all had to catch colds now is anyone's guess. Are you listening God?*

I know there are a lot of things goin' on in this world which need your attention. But really – did Girly Girl have to get such a whopper of a cold a week before graduation? Her nose is on fire and chapped, her cheeks horribly mottled. Graduation robes don't have pockets for tissues you know.)

And they play *Pomp and Circumstance*, which I have always frankly disliked, and the auditorium of parents watch a slide show of our kids over the years – which makes everyone reach for the tissues in *their* pockets. And we sit there - almost, but not nearly, in as much shock as twenty-two years ago when that doctor told us, in the kindest voice possible, that there was a little something special about our baby.

A little bit different – though a baby still, ready to cuddle and care for and love.

Shell-shocked twenty-two years ago we left the hospital and took those babies home.

And now, shell-shocked we leave the auditorium; keeping an eye on our graduates who aren't going off to University in the fall, who aren't registered for summer courses to get a head start on college; who aren't taking off with a group of friends to road trip it and discover America. Or, what I longed to do when I was eighteen (or twenty-two), head to Europe, duffle bag in hand, making the most of youth hostels and mass transit; and my own feet.

Our Girl won't do those things. Our Girl will go home to cake, ice cream, and balloons; warm hugs and reassuring exclamations of *"Yes! You Graduated!"*

Then she'll grab that balloon bouquet, snag a can of coke, and haul her little, stubborn, opinionated self upstairs to her lair; and *Abba* or *Queen* will soon be blasting from beneath her firmly closed door.

And Scott and I sit still for a bit. I look over the notes I've jotted down these past few months

Girly Girl: Activities

 Bowling

Dance

Exercise

Homeschool?

Business?

And I realize one more millionth time that we don't *have* a business to involve Girly Girl in and what the crap is she gonna do with her days? How is she to feel productive and fulfilled?

And I won't be one of those sad eyed old people hauling around a forty year old adult child looking lonely and confused and depressed as hell!

I know Scott's words before he utters them:

We aren't like that. You're not like that. Girly Girl has flair and opinion and energy.

And I say yeal; and we get up and hang curtains and paint and plan what to do next.

But still that post graduation list haunts my desk. A sorry, paltry list of five items, a few question marks, and too many dots...

 I don't look at it.

And I don't flip the calendar ahead to September. My favorite: golden, fiery Fall.

Autumn leaves are too dazzling to even glance at right now.

The thought of Autumn stings my eyes; making them tear.

Girly Girl's Resume

Well, it has finally happened.

After nineteen years of public school, Our Girl graduated from "her college" yesterday, *forever and ever and always.*

 This has come as the longest, most drawn out, totally in denial, sudden, and utter shock *ever.*

I'm doing much better than I'd imagined I would. Scott hasn't said a whole lot – so I suppose he's ok as well. (Or perhaps in a catatonic state. I haven't quite decided yet.)

Personally I don't become catatonic. I yell. A lot.

At any rate, now is the time (well, perhaps after a summer off for good behaviour) for Girly Girl to venture out into the big, possibly mean, uber frightening world and forge her own path!

She's always been a great little path forger.

She's forged paths into her brother's rooms to ~~filch~~ *borrow* any spare change they had lying around (obviously they weren't using it); to snag spare cd's or dvd's.

(Hey – it certainly wasn't her who left the cupboard unlocked!)

To spirit away a case of coke which really no one seemed to need at all; and to *disappear from her middle school entirely* one terrifying day only to found at a convenience store/gas station down the street enjoying a fountain drink and a large bag of cheetos which she had no money to pay for.

So, once her summer sabbatical comes to its end, The Girl will be forced to choose amongst the many positions she will no doubt be offered.

(We're considering getting her own mail box. Or perhaps smartly uniformed postal workers will haul in bag after bag of mail, like in those old 40's movies I love so much.)

And here, you lucky readers you, is a sneak peak at Girly Girl's qualifications.

Her resume if you will. Take a peak and sigh with wonder and more than a hint of jealously at what one awfully short girl can accomplish in a scant 22 years.

Name: Girly Girl Taylor

Home Address: The Lair, Witt's End On The Rock in the Wild Wild West

Phone #: *I've never cared for the phone, except for those ~~two~~ three times I dialed 911 when I was 4. The police came immediately. It was most gratifying, and I felt I had done my duty in keeping our local force on their toes.*

Job Applying For: *Unlike most other poor sods, I have many talents. Thus the list of possibilities is rather long, though totally fascinating:*

Dancer– *from hip hop to step dance I can do it all. I have broken my bed several times practicing the leaps and bounds my art requires, but that is the sacrifice one makes. (Plus Daddy always fixes it.)*

Singer – *Just ask my brothers. I can hit notes higher and louder than any stereo and speaker system ANYWHERE.*

Actress- *I am able to re-enact a myriad of films: from Jackie Chan films to ANNIE* to all three JURASSIC PARKS . My evading the velocitators in the kitchen scene is especially breathtaking.*

(*It is a little know fact that ANNIE was created especially for me. Really. TOTAL FACT.)

Closet Cleaner-Outer - *I can clean out a closet quicker than Mary Poppins (whom, by the way, I am also fully adapt at re-enacting)*

*You don't **want** your closet cleaned out and rearranged you say? Au Contraire. Of course you do! You just don't realize you do – wait till I surprise you! You'll be thrilled.*

Rolling my "R"'s- *I can roll my R's faster and longer than any person alive. Really. My mom is considering calling the Guinness Book of World Records. It's absolutely amazing.*

To move closer to God is to move closer to everything, both joy and sorrow, light and darkness.

~Parker Palmer

Our Girl at Disneyland. Huggin' on those friendly bears!

Girly Girl's Resume   Part II

On obtaining a first class ticket to New York...

The Girl is currently saving money in order to pursue her dream job of working at the Natural History Museum in New York. She is looking forward to meeting her hero, Teddy Roosevelt, when he comes alive at night.

(Yes this is a bit worrisome and I am still considering contacting the airports.)

For this endeavour Girly Girl needs MONEY; a continuing list of the occupations for which she is uniquely qualified follows:

Pilfering: Our Girl can do a slight of hand which would make the Artful Dodger green with jealousy. And she has the little innocent *Who Me?* look down to perfection. No one would the suspect this Girl of doing anything sneaky and cunning. Oh how wrong they'd be...

CIA Agent: For all of the above reasons. Girly Girl would be the perfect person to smuggle something across enemy lines. The mean, hairy customs person would take one look at her angelic little face, stamp her passport and let her through the gate. And Our Girl would easily deliver the microfilm or computer chip or whatever, so long as she didn't become distracted by an intriguing looking shop or a McDonalds.

Folder of Laundry: Girly Girl is the greatest dang laundry folder the world has ever known. For years now she's been refolding the laundry I've folded, since I apparently do it completely wrong. Her drawers are beautiful, organized displays Martha Stewart would envy.

Cook: Specialty Dishes- popcorn, toast, popcorn soup soggy mac & cheese (recipes already included.) Though she sets a table beautifully and loves broccoli, which I think is an indication of great character.

Making Gingerbread Houses

We are formed and molded by our thoughts. Those whose minds are shaped by selfless thoughts give joy when they speak or act. Joy follows them like a shadow that never leaves them.

~Buddah

The Wilderness Path II

The Wilderness Path, where Joy follows like a shadow.

And touching the *millaire,* the milestones, along the way.

It is a daily pilgrimage, this life of ours. Are you aware of it? And do you notice them, the *millaire*, the milestones, which we pass? The ancients of Rome embedded an untold number of such markers into the earth; to lead the way, to mark the miles, the borders, the dominance of Rome. Fashioned of stone, perhaps of wood, their carved markings now faded and worn; the wood they were crafted from long since rotted away. They served their purpose, for a time; and then time moved on.

The millaire along the Wilderness Path cannot be seen with the human eye. But they exist, and are eternal.

They sparkle in the evening and morning sun for those who seek the light and who chose to notice them. They are there to be touched lightly while passing, or to rest against when the Wilderness Path has become too tiresome to bear.

And it is sometimes so tiresome, isn't it? The burdens heavy and cumbersome. And people *will ask* things of you which you have neither the strength nor inclination to fulfill. Petty requests, mundane questions, comments or complaints which, if you are forced to listen to *just one more time*, you will claw your face and rake your hair and run screaming...*screaming...*

Out into the Wilderness?

The Wilderness Time. And the path through it. Follow the path, and Joy will follow you like a shadow.

Empty

Last night was one of those rare times when my house, aside from the dogs and I, stood empty.

It was amazingly creepy.

For I tend to be a fanciful person, I see flashes of shadow people from the corner of my eye, I hear noises which by anyone more grounded than myself would seem to be the house "settling", I am convinced whenever Mimsy growls at *something* outside the window, at *something* in the corner (which for the life of me I cannot see at all), that there is indeed something there. Visible only to her canine senses, impossible for my eyes to detect.

And I wonder, during those rare moments, what I shall do when Someday arrives. That horrible, long dreaded and ignored Someday: when the house is indeed empty but for the dogs and myself.

(And perhaps Girly Girl. But I can't image our busy author of the creepy *missives* (*They're in my closet...*) being of much practical help at all.)

That Someday when Scott will be at work, Girly Girl will be busy with her Girly Girl activities, my boys will be grown and off living their lives, pursuing their dreams and though just a phone call, a skype away in our ultra connected world, not *Here*. And Witt's End will stand (mostly) empty but for myself and my dogs and their growls directed into empty corners.

So now I prepare to fill that emptiness. For, along with fanciful, I am a glass half full kinda person. A *fill that glass till it's brimming over, flooding the joy and laughter and life across the counter, down the cupboards, across the floor.*

(I'll trip those shadow people up, I'll rinse out those dark corners, (dust bunnies damp tailed and in retreat.)

Working on filling that fearful, future emptiness. With words and colors, peace and growth.

Well watered from my half full and filling glass.

Hunkering Down

I'm in panic mode these days.
There's a storm out there; wild and fierce. I can smell it and feel the wind bite. Last night I watched the sky: pink streaked and grey low lying cumulus clouds with a silver brilliance behind them so bright it hurt my eyes.

These are the times when you hunker down.

When you stack the wood high in its warmer, dry place, and stoke the fire till sparks flare from the chimney in a whirling, dancing, frenzy; watching as those few escape, skipping to the ground. Dying to a dark fizzle upon the snow; then melting away.

(Though you can spy the black spot there amidst the white; if you dare look.)
The warm blankets and cups of tea or cocoa; break baking just cause we can while I stack the books deep.

They are a guard wall these books. A fortress, an ocean; and we are upon an island in the midst of all this where the voices fail to penetrate, (though the whispers of the wind are audible. And we listen and try to decipher and understand.)

And I am hidden. Protected. Held fast in spell bound words so deep I would struggle to reach the surface even if I wanted to.

There are too many things to do now. Too many arms pulling, too many fists raised; cares too deep and troubles too ancient. The gusts of air they carry along are toxic. So I hold my breath and strengthen my island. Sweet, soft breezes filled with baking bread, warm pastries, and savory stews waft about the books, the stacks and stacks of papers thick with words, the latched doors, and floors swept clean.

Hunkering down. Preparing, arming, resting, centering.

The winds whisper and bite; scattering wild dancing chimney sparks. Red, black, and winking, they flow before my moving eyes like an incoming tide. And I don't blink.

Not even once.

Obstacles cannot crush me. Every obstacle yields to stern resolve. He who is fixed to a star does not change his mind.

~Leonardo Da Vinci

Good Day Prayers

I hate to admit it, but much too often I forget about these kind of prayers.

During the trying times, the testing times; those hard turns and sudden pitfalls along the *Wilderness Path* the prayers come easily don't they? Those fall on your knees, face in your hands, or lifted, beseeching, toward the heavens moments. Tear streaked, pain wracked, gut wounded minutes, hours, days, weeks, or even months of pain and prayer and seeking help.

What about the Good Days. Because surely they're sprinkled in, either thick and heavy or sparse and light, along your Path.

(May all our moments be thick and heavy with Good Day sprinkles.)

Do you remember the Good Day Prayers? I've been trying to – but it's hard.

In between the baskets of laundry which pile up endlessly, awaiting folding. The chest cold which arrives with a sudden vengeance despite the errands I must still accomplish (coughing and popping cough drops like an addict all the while.) The dinners, the dishes, the invasion of thousands upon thousands of box elder beetles which have hit this year and must be battled daily as I pray for a long, hard freeze.

Is such prayer a Good Day Prayer? I think not.

But there *are* times when I remember.

We watched *The Sandlot* last Sunday. And each of us, from my twenty-two year old college senior, (that guy always stretched for time), to my nine year old enjoyed it with that same simple pleasure we used to watch movies. (*Aladdin,* the newest *Narnia,* whatever Disney Classic I'd listed on the Sunday night schedule for that week.) And I found myself watching my children *(oh I can't quite say men, not yet),* laughing and eating ice cream, more than I watched the film itself.

And I knew*: this is a Good Day Prayer.*

And there are more:

Smelling the wild little guy smell on the back of Little Bit's neck after he's been outside to play.

Folding their clothes: those now so soft "Red Baron" sweat pants bought for Son&Heir years ago, searching in vain for sock matches, wondering how many towels, if any, we own without at least one hole.

Trying a new recipe, wondering who'll say "yuck" and ask for peanut butter instead. (No they won't get it.) Falling back on an old standby, wondering who'll say "Oh my gosh not that again." (They'll eat it anyway.)

Watching Curlytop make eggs for lunch yet again. Coyote create his "signature rolls."

Girly-Girl changes her clothes at least five times a day whilst blithely tossing the ones she "doesn't care for today" into the hamper, still folded.

Good Times Prayers all. Frustrating, messy, infuriating at times.

But *(Thankfully,Thankfullly...)* not one fear ridden moment among them. No swollen eyes or trembling lips, no white knuckled fist clenched against my stomach so I'm still able to stand and remember to breathe.

So I'm watching close for those Good Time Prayer moments.

Spreading those sprinkles as thick as I'm able.

Never even thinking to ask for a cherry on top.

And The Dance Continues...

The Dancing Chromosomes.
Never can you be certain how they will align, how they will pair up, how the dance will flow.

Girly Girl has Trisomy 21, the most common form of Down Syndrome – she has an extra 21st chromosome, in every single one of the cells of her body.

What does that extra chromosome contain, really? Extra information yes. Enough to cause some confusion, some breakdown or muddled knowledge from cell to cell as they interact; whispering their own private language to which none of us are privy, yet upon which each of us relies – though we never even pause to think of it.

So, is Our Girl confused by life? Sometimes. Is she more easily frightened, or angered, or frustrated? Yes.

But then aren't we all, to some extent.

Have you heard the saying, I'm sorry I cannot remember the author, that *a society is judged by how it treats its weakest members? The young, the old, the handicapped.*

How do you think we're doing?
I don't think Our Girl wastes her time pondering such questions. She doesn't realize the meaning of the word "handicapped", much less bother to apply it to herself. Of course she is a different – Princesses are different, and she is most certainly a Princess. And, as I said, it's a pretty good gig – if you can get it.

Long nights I have wondered and wandered.
And I've come to ask myself, to ask the universe, to ask God (*he is listening, don't you think?*): Why? And How?

And what really, does that extra chromosome contain? Extra information yes. But also perhaps an extra, oh so tiny, bit of the spark.

All cells contain this spark: energy, the light, the touch of God's finger, the soul.

The Human Soul.

What is it if not the spark which sets each of our cells going; that which makes our cells alive. The cells form and multiply, coalesce and get moving, creating... *Us.*

So, that extra chromosome, that extra tiny bit of spark which Our Girl has in every solitary cell, is it *that* which bathes her in the light?

Golden it is. Silver edged; tinted pale with peach and rose. Oh so easy to see if only one's eyes and heart and mind are open.

The extra, dancing chromosome. Aligning itself, flittering away, flowing back again. The light about it glows and breaks. Just as Our Girl glows, basking in the light.

Open your eyes, gaze into the light. It is there for all and filled with love.

But be careful: it is dazzling, and so much dazzling love will almost surely break your heart.

Wishing the Brightest of Blessings to you and yours along this journey,

Girly Girl, Son & Heir, Curlytop, Coyote, Little Bit, Scott, and Lisa.

Girly Girl – loaded with Wiggles loot!

~About The Author~

Lisa D.B. Taylor

(no one is quite certain what the initials D.B. stand for — though most, I among them, suspect Diabolically Brilliant),

lives, writes, and regularly breathes at her oversized home in the hills where she thinks about exercising, does an amazing amount of laundry, and watches the deer nibble away the costly plants and trees she has painstakingly planted.

Said oversized home is fondly christened Witt's End Upon the Rock.
The name is self-explanatory and entirely true.

Self-described as Perpetually Overwhelmed & Understaffed, Lisa is the mother of five children; each of whom has evidently inherited her talkative nature and none of their father's reticence.

Thus Witt's End is a noisy, rather chaotic, and admittedly messy place.

The family also keeps chickens, one guinea hen, and several dogs.
*Lisa enjoys travel, chocolate, hot tea and sweet, reading, blogging at **Its Own Sweet Will.neebeep.com** and, naturally, not having to cook dinner.*

Fantasizing about sliding into her size 5 jeans one fine, future day also occupies an inordinate amount of her time.

Other books by L.D.B. Taylor currently available:
Reclamation: A Heartbroken & Then I Got Better Love Story (The early days of Girly Girl's journey.)

And the **Life at Witt's End: On The Edge & Teetering In The Wild West West** series:

Guilty Admissions (Also Weird Stuff Which Has Happened To My Mother, Featuring The Attic Man)

Whispers & Traditions

&

Trust Me. I Know Stuff.

~Share The Light & Share The Wealth~

See ya next time!

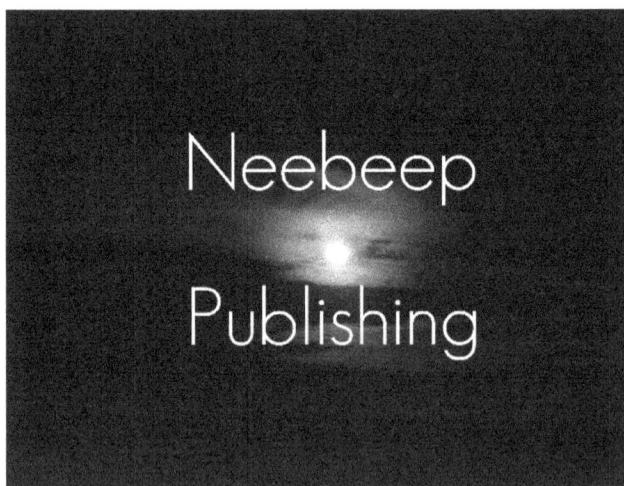

Neebeep.com

www.ingramcontent.com/pod-product-compliance
Lightning Source LLC
Chambersburg PA
CBHW020516030426

42337CB00011B/416